The New Novello Choral Edition

JOSEPH HAYDN

Nelson Mass
Missa in Angustiis (Hob. XXII/11)

for soprano, alto, tenor and bass soloists, SATB chorus, organ and orchestra

Vocal score

Revised by Michael Pilkington (2000 and 2004)

Order No: NOV 072513

NOVELLO PUBLISHING LIMITED

Cover illustration: first page of the Kyrie from Haydn's *Missa in Angustiis* Hob.XXII/11, copied by Haydn's copyist Johann Elssler (BM Add. MS31711, reproduced courtesy of the British Library)

PREFACE

Haydn composed six settings of the Mass text for the name day of Princess Maria Josepha Hemengild Esterházy. The *Nelson Mass* is the third of these, written between 10 July and 31 August 1798. Originally simply entitled *Missa*, Haydn gave it the title *Missa in Angustiis* in his own catalogue of works. Although a literal translation of 'augustiis' is 'limited' – restricted, in terms of time or space, or of money and supplies – it has been variously interpreted in this context as 'Mass in time of affliction, in anxiety and danger'[1] and 'Mass in Time of Fear'[2]. Haydn's use of 'angustiis' as 'Mass in straitened circumstances' might well be a reference to the fact that at the time he was composing the mass he had no woodwind instruments available, since Prince Esterházy had temporarily disbanded his wind players.

The better known title of *Nelson Mass* was applied to the work quite early, probably because Admiral Nelson and Emma Hamilton attended a performance of the Mass while staying at Eisenstadt as a guest of Prince Esterházy in September 1800. The popular idea that the Mass was composed in celebration of Nelson's victory at the battle of the Nile in 1798 is contradicted by the dates; the battle was fought between 1-3 of August, and the news did not reach Vienna until mid-September. Many old English scores carry the title *Imperial Mass*, based on the extraordinary claim in an early French edition that the work was composed for the coronation of Joseph II that had taken place in 1765!

The original scoring is for three trumpets[3], timpani, strings and organ. Unusually, Haydn has written out many passages for the organ in full, rather than merely providing a figured bass. Robbins Landon considers the unusual absence of wind instruments to be intentional, suggesting that Haydn could have obtained any necessary players from Vienna. On the other hand, Thomas quotes a letter from Georg August Griesinger[4] to Härtel in Leipzig saying that Haydn had 'given the wind parts to the organ, because at that time Prince Esterházy had disbanded the wind players.' In the same letter Griesinger passes on an instruction from Haydn 'to transfer all the obbligato material of the organ part to the wind instruments, and to have the work printed in this form.' Breitkopf and Härtel duly published the Mass in 1803, with parts for flute, two oboes and two bassoons, and rewriting the third trumpet as an obbligato part in nearly all the movements. This version was possibly by August Eberhard Müller[5]. A different set of wind parts, for flute, two oboes, two clarinets, bassoon and two horns exists in the Esterházy archives at Eisenstadt, perhaps by Johann Nepomuk Fuchs, Haydn's successor (according to Thomas, who gives them in small print), or Hummel (Robbins Landon's supposition). Some other sources have optional wind parts of their own.

The present edition provides Breitkopf and Härtel's wind parts, but restores the original third trumpet part in place of that printed by them. Performances with organ and no woodwind present the music as written by Haydn, but Griesinger's letter seems to justify use of wind parts if desired. If the wind parts are used, the organ may either play continuo or be omitted altogether. The reduction of the score made by Berthold Tours for the previous Novello edition was based on the Breitkopf and Härtel score, and has here been modified to match the original version without wind parts.

This edition is based on the score in the British Library, Add. MS 31711, generally considered a fair copy made by Johann Elssler, Haydn's personal copyist. Strangely, the title page lists the instruments as published by Breitkopf and Härtel, though the actual score contains the obbligato organ part and no woodwind. At some date after the first performance, Haydn made some alterations in the solo parts, and carefully inserted them into his autograph, deleting the original version. These changes are included in the British Library copy and are followed here. If Haydn had made these adjustments solely for a particular set of soloists it is unlikely he would have taken the trouble to delete the older version in his manuscript.

Michael Pilkington
Old Coulsdon, 2000

NOTES

1   Günter Thomas; preface to Joseph Haydn *Missa in Angustiis*, Hob.XXII/11 (Bärenreiter, 1979)
2   H.C. Robbins Landon; preface to Joseph Haydn *Missa in Angustiis*, Hob.XXII/11 (Eulenburg, 1979)
3   Robbins Landon suggests that it might well be that the third trumpet part, appearing only in the Kyrie and Benedictus, was intended for as many spare players as were available at the time.
4   Georg August Griesinger (1769-1845). German diplomat and writer. He was Haydn's biographer and confidant. He negotiated with Haydn on behalf of Breitkopf and Härtel. His letters to Härtel contain valuable information on Haydn's last years.
5   August Eberhard Müller (1767-1817). Conductor, flautist, organist and composer. He performed many works by Mozart and Haydn, prepared piano arrangements for Breitkopf and Härtel (including one for *The Creation*) and advised on their publication of the first complete editions of those composers' works.

NOTES

Dynamic markings in square brackets and slurs with 'cuts' are editorial suggestions, and are provided for consistency; however it is not assumed that repeated passages are required to have the same phrasing.

Sources

MS	British Library Add. MS 31711
Landon	Joseph Haydn, Missa in Angustiis, Hob. XXII, ed. H. C. Robbins Landon (Eulenburg, 1963)
Thomas	Joseph Haydn, Missa in Angustiis, Hob. XXII, ed. Günter Thomas (Bärenreiter, 1979)
Tours	Joseph Haydn, Nelson Mass, ed. Berthold Tours (Novello, 1880s)

Kyrie

Solo passages for all voices other than the principal soprano should be sung by members of the choir.

b.85	The last semiquaver in RH (second violin) is an f in MS, but at b.118 it is an e. Thomas gives f in both places, Landon and Tours e in both places. The e seems the more satisfactory solution.
b.143	The tenor and bass parts shown in this bar are from MS; they are given by Thomas with the note 'voices tacet in the authentic copies', but not in any other edition. Bearing in mind the orchestral tutti starting in this bar this may well be an afterthought by the composer.

Credo

b.31	Haydn omitted to set the words 'Et in unum Dominum Jesum Christum, Filium Dei unigenitum' at this point.
b.169	Haydn omitted to set the words 'qui ex patre Filioque procedit' at this point.

Sanctus

Originally bb. 2 and 5 had pause marks, and bb. 3 and 6 were not present, given thus by Landon and Thomas; however, these bars are not only given in Breitkopf and Härtel but also in MS

b.13	No tempo mark in MS or Thomas, but see bar b.136 of Benedictus.

Benedictus

bb.122-8	The timpani notes given in brackets come from Breitkopf and Härtel, are noted by Thomas and Landon as appearing in one set of parts, but do not appear in MS.

★★★★

The previous Novello edition of the *Nelson Mass* (NOV070161) was based on the faulty Breitkopf and Härtel edition of 1803, which contained many errors, mostly to do with the text, its underlay, dynamics and phrase marks. You will find a list of these errors in the Appendix (p. 85). The new edition follows Haydn's score as presented in the first three sources given above (see Preface).

The new edition matches the old page for page, so that they may easily be studied together.

NELSON MASS

KYRIE

4

6

*see Preface

*see Preface

SOPRANO SOLO

GLORIA

SOPRANO SOLO

Pax_____ ho — mi — ni-bus,

— mi — ni-bus, et in____

et in — ter — ra pax ho-

ter — ra pax ho — mi-ni-bus bo — — næ vo — — —

— mi — ni-bus bo — — næ, bo — — næ vo — — lun —

— — lun — ta — tis, bo — — nae vo — lun —

— ta — — tis, bo — næ vo — lun — ta — — — —

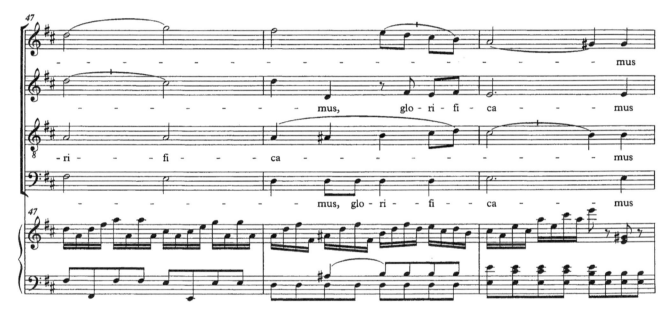

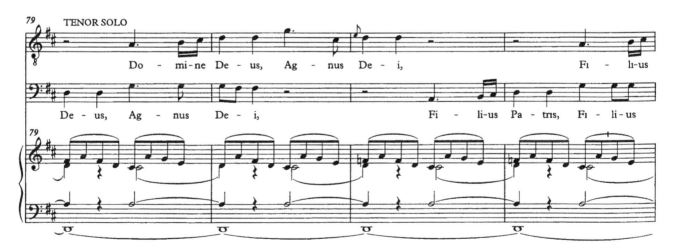

QUONIAM TU SOLUS

CREDO

ET INCARNATUS

ET RESURREXIT

*Bass notes 6, 7 = B, B in sources

*see Preface

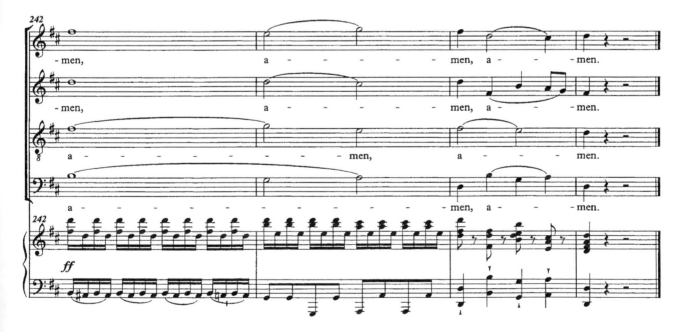

SANCTUS

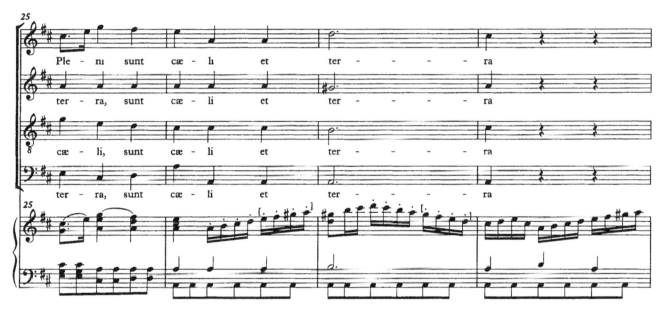

BENEDICTUS

64

no - mi - ne Do - mi - ni. Be - ne - dic - tus qui

ve - nit in no - - - - mi - ne Do - mi - ni,

in no - - - - - - -

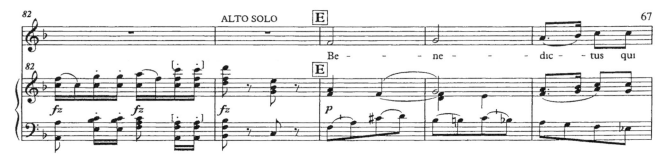

AGNUS DEI

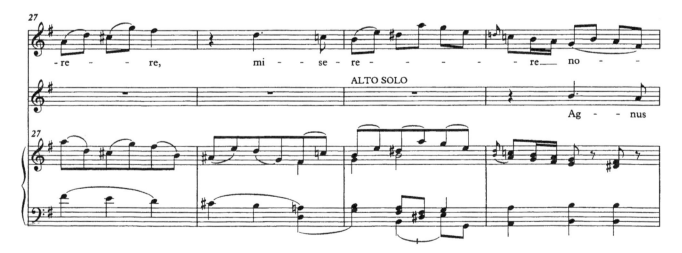

DONA NOBIS

APPENDIX

A list of alterations made to the earlier Novello edition of the *Nelson Mass* vocal score (NOV070161) corrected in the new edition

SOPRANO SOLO

Kyrie

33

- lei - son

107   Has music of Chorus Soprano (in error)

Gloria

5

Glo - ri - a in ex -

68

Pa - ter om - ni - po -

Quoniam

175

so-lus Al - tis - si - mus.

178-79

Je - su Chris - te,

238   Beat 2 'Tutti'
243   Beat 3 'Solo'

Et resurrexit

205

sæ - cu - li

Benedictus

56

Be - ne -

ALTO SOLO

Quoniam

238   Beat 2 'Tutti'
242   Beat 1 'Solo'

Benedictus

89

Do - mi -

TENOR SOLO

Gloria

18-19

ter - ra pax ho - mi - ni - bus

23-24

ter - ra pax ho - mi - ni - bus,

81

De - i,

Quoniam

238   Beat 2 'Tutti'
242   Beat 3 'Solo'

Agnus Dei

37

no - bis

BASS SOLO
Quoniam

| 238 | Beat 2 'Tutti' |
| 241 | Beat 3 'Solo' |

Chorus SOPRANO
Kyrie

33   Ky - ri - e

| 77 | Second beat has accent |

77   underlay son, e -

| 123 | No '*sfz*' on beat 1 |
| 124 | No '*sfz*' on beat 1 |

156-59   underlay (e -) - lei - - - son.

Gloria

| 33 | '*p*' on beat 2 |
| 33 | Accent on beat 3 |

33   underlay Lau - da - mus

| 36 | Accent on beat 3 |

36   underlay a - do - ra - mus

38	'*cresc.*' on beat 2
42	'*fz*' followed by *diminuendo* hairpin on beat 3
43	'*fz*' followed by *diminuendo* hairpin on beat 3
44	'*fz*' followed by *diminuendo* hairpin on beat 3
45	'*fz*' followed by *diminuendo* hairpin on beat 3

Qui tollis

| 167 | '*cresc.*' |
| 168 | '*f*' |

168-70   underlay no - - bis

Quoniam

219-22   underlay Pa - tris, A - - - - - men,

| 238 | Beat 2 'Tutti' |
| 243 | Beat 3 'Solo' |

Credo

13-14   underlay - ni - po - ten - tem, Fac -

74-77   underlay - scen - dit de cœ - lis,

Et resurrexit

140   ter - ti - a di - e se -

| 213 | Tacet until b.214 |

228-30   underlay (a) - - - - men

| 237–39 | underlay | (a) - - - - men |

Sanctus

1	dynamics	*sf* < >
4	dynamics	*sf* < >
21–24	underlay	glo - ri - a tu - - a,
31–50	'Hosanna'

Benedictus

| 132 | Do - mi - |

Dona nobis

49	underlay	Do - na pa - cem
54	pa - -
56	- cem pa -
61	underlay	no - bis, do - na

Chorus ALTO

Kyrie
77	Second beat has accent
123	No '*sfz*' on beat 1
124	No '*sfz*' on beat 1

Gloria
33	'*p*' on beat 2
33	Accent on beat 3
33	underlay	Lau - da - mus
36	Accent on beat 3
36	underlay	a - do - ra - mus
38	'*cresc.*' on beat 2
42	'*fz*' followed by *diminuendo* hairpin on beat 3
43	'*fz*' followed by *diminuendo* hairpin on beat 3
44	'*fz*' followed by *diminuendo* hairpin on beat 3
45	'*fz*' followed by *diminuendo* hairpin on beat 3

Qui tollis
167	'*cresc.*'
168	'*f*'
168–70	underlay	no - - bis

Quoniam
218–20	underlay	Pa - tris, A - men, A - men, A -
238	Beat 2 'Tutti'
243	Beat 1 'Solo'

Credo

14–15 underlay -ni - po -ten - tem, Fac -

74–77 underlay cœ - lis, de -scen -dit de cœ - lis,

Et resurrexit

237–39 underlay (a) - - men, A - men,

Sanctus

1 dynamics *sf* < >

4 dynamics *sf* < >

31–50 'Hosanna'

Benedictus

96 - dic - tus qui

120 Do - mi -

Dona nobis

49–50 underlay no -bis pa -cem, pa - -

54–55 do - na no - bis____ pa -

60–61 underlay do -na no -bis pa -cem, do -na

83 underlay do - na

116 underlay (pa) - cem, pa -

Chorus TENOR

Kyrie
77   Second beat has accent
123 No '*sfz*' on beat 1
124 No '*sfz*' on beat 1
143 Optional entry not included
Gloria
33   '*p*' on beat 2
33   Accent on beat 3
33   underlay Lau - da - mus

36   Accent on beat 3
36   underlay a - do - ra - mus

42–45 *diminuendo* hairpin on beat 3
46   '*f*' on beat 4

Qui tollis

167	'cresc.'
168	'*f*'
168-70	underlay no – – bis

Quoniam

229	Beat 1 C♮ (and in accompaniment)
238	Beat 2 'Tutti'
242	Beat 3 'Solo'

Credo

13-14   underlay
-ni – po – ten – tem, Fac –

74-77   underlay
-scen – dit de cœ – lis,_____

79
cœ – lis, de

Et resurrexit

152-53   underlay
mor – tu – os, et

192
-tis – ma in re – mis – si

214
vi – tam

227-28   underlay
– men, A – –

Sanctus

1   dynamics
sf < >

4   dynamics
sf < >

9
De – us__ Sa – ba –

18   underlay
– ra

19-22   underlay
glo – ri – a tu – – a,

31-50   'Hosanna'

Benedictus

102
no – mi – ne

132
Do – mi –

Dona nobis

76-77   underlay
pa – – cem.

94   underlay
no – bis pa – cem,

Chorus BASS

Kyrie

77   Second beat has accent

123   No '*sfz*' on beat 1

124   No '*sfz*' on beat 1

143   Optional entry not included

150   underlay   (elei) - son, e

Gloria

33   '*p*' on beat 2

33   Accent on beat 3

33   underlay   Lau - da - mus

36   Accent on beat 3

36   underlay   a - do - ra - mus

42-45   *diminuendo* hairpin on beat 3

Qui tollis

167   '*cresc.*'

168   '*f*'

168-70   underlay   no - - bis

Quoniam

238   Beat 2 'Tutti'

241   Beat 3 'Solo'

Credo

14-15   underlay   - ni - po - ten - tem, Fac -

74-77   underlay   cœ - lis, de - scen - dit de cœ - lis,

Sanctus

1   dynamics   *sf* < >

4   dynamics   *sf* < >

18   underlay   - ra

19-22   underlay   glo - ri - a tu - - a,

25-26   underlay   ter - ra, et ter - ra, et

31-50   'Hosanna'

Dona nobis

65-66   - cem,

[b.65 beat 2 - b.66 beat 1 tacet]